LANARKSHIRE'S LAST DAYS (

by
W.A.C. Smith

Set in a smoky corner of Coatbridge, the usual pollution at grimy Langloan Station was made worse on 20 June, 1961, by this class 4MT 2-6-4T, no. 42201. It was running in under a pall of smoke at the head of a train which, one hour and thirty-five minutes earlier, had left Balloch on the bonnie banks of Loch Lomond!

© W.A.C. Smith, 2000
First published in the United Kingdom, 2000,
by Stenlake Publishing, Ochiltree Sawmill, The Lade,
Ochiltree, Ayrshire, KA18 2NX
Telephone / Fax: 01290 423114
www.stenlake.co.uk

ISBN 1 84033 127 5

All photographs by W.A.C. Smith

More glamorous motive power could, however, be seen on occasions at Langloan. A two week programme of 'Excursions by Historic Locomotives' for the Scottish Industries Exhibition at Glasgow's Kelvin Hall commenced on 5 September, 1959, and a quartet of preserved Scottish locomotives (today to be seen in the Glasgow Museum of Transport) were joined in this programme by the former Great Western Railway 4-4-0, no. 3440, 'City of Truro', which had been credited with a record breaking 102 m.p.h. in 1904. This engine is seen here passing Langloan Junction punctually at 12.28 p.m. on 19 September, piloted by a North British Railway 4-4-0, no. 256, 'Glen Douglas', with an 8.30 a.m. special from Aberdeen to Glasgow (Central).

INTRODUCTION

Lanarkshire witnessed both the birth of the steam locomotive and its death. The Garnkirk & Glasgow Railway was opened in 1831 and used primitive steam locomotives to provide passenger and goods services on a double track, initiating the transition from the crude horse-drawn waggonways which had formed adjuncts to coal pits and canals. Along with the Wishaw & Coltness and Clydesdale Railways, and by now renamed the Glasgow, Garnkirk & Coatbridge Railway (and with a change of gauge from 4 feet 6 inches to the standard 4 feet and 8½ inches), it enabled the Caledonian Railway coming up from Carlisle and over Beattock summit in Dumfriesshire to reach Glasgow. This route (part of today's electrified West Coast Main Line) was opened in 1848, forking at Carstairs to reach Edinburgh.

The rival North British Railway had a monopoly in the Monklands, but sporadic attempts to penetrate further into Lanarkshire met with little success and, with the Glasgow & South Western Railway kept at bay in Ayrshire, the county was to remain a Caley stronghold.

The railways sparked an industrial revolution in Lanarkshire with lines proliferating throughout the nineteenth century and briefly into the twentieth, the last of significance being the Lanarkshire & Ayrshire from Newton to Ardrossan completed in 1903 and the mid-Lanark lines around Strathaven and Coalburn which opened in 1905. By the 1930s branches were closing as passengers were lured away by the bus, which itself would be replaced by the family car which brought with it all the consequent problems with traffic congestion and pollution.

Changing economic factors following upon the First World War had brought about the government-inspired railway grouping of 1923 with a plethora of private companies (123 in all) reduced by amalgamation to just four: London, Midland & Scottish, London & North Eastern, Great Western, and Southern. After the Second World War these were brought into public ownership, under the title of British Railways, and divided into five regions until privatisation returned fifty years later.

For a time following upon nationalisation in 1948 steam continued to

Right: A class Y9 0-4-0 saddle tank, no. 68123, prepares to do a little shunting at the North British Tube Works of Stewarts & Lloyds Ltd at Coatbridge on the evening of 18 June, 1959. These diminutive locomotives were a Neilson & Co. design dating from 1882 and belied their archaic appearance by an ability to get into remote corners of docks, factories and ironworks. The North British Railway had thirty-five of them, the last remaining in service with British Railways until 1962.

reign supreme on British railways, but the government-funded Modernisation Plan of 1955 with its emphasis on diesel and electric traction was the beginning of the end. Not only were no steam locomotives built after 1959, but relatively new examples already in service and costed to remain so until the year 2000 were scrapped in what can now be seen as shocking waste of public money. Meanwhile, the system itself was ruthlessly pruned by Dr Beeching in the mistaken belief that by chopping off not only branches but also main lines, the remaining trunk routes could be made viable.

The last scheduled steam passenger working within the Scottish Region of British Railways took place on 28 April, 1967, from Gourock to Glasgow, and although occasional forays north of the border continued to be made until the end of that year by London Midland Region locomotives based at Carlisle's Kingmoor depot, this effectively brought to an end 136 years of steam traction on Scotland's railways. On Britain's railways as a whole steam ended in August, 1968.

Thanks to the dedication of railway enthusiasts, steam locomotives can today be seen on preserved railways and working special trains on selected main lines, but what can never be recreated are the everyday and everywhere scenes pictured in the following pages.

On 12 April, 1956, a class N2 0-6-2T, no. 69596, comes off the old Monkland and Kirkintilloch line at Sunnyside Junction at Coatbridge, bound for Kipps with empty wagons from Gunnie Yard. These locomotives were used on London suburban services and were a not too successful import following the 1923 railway grouping.

Kipps Motive Power Depot, situated on the Bathgate line at the east end of Coatbridge, latterly housed some forty-five locomotives, mainly former North British Railway types for working mineral traffic to and from the once numerous ironworks and collieries in the area. This photograph, taken on 30 April, 1960, shows a J36 0-6-0, no. 65249 (built in 1892 and modified in 1916), and a J35, no. 64534 (dating from 1913), both very typical of the period. The shed, which also had several V3 and N2 tank locos used for passenger work on the Queen Street Low Level line, closed in 1963.

The class 7P Britannia Pacific, no. 70041, was named 'Sir John Moore' when built in 1951, but by the dying days of steam had been shorn of its nameplates as it calls at Coatbridge (Central) with the 9.25 a.m. from Crewe to Perth on 5 March, 1966. The station had been rebuilt in lavish style by the Caledonian Railway for, in addition to through trains serving Birmingham, London (Euston), Perth and Inverness, there were local trains between Glasgow (Buchanan Street) and Hamilton as well as to those from Glasgow Central Low Level. However, the station's present day state of dilapidation may well make this hard to believe!

On a wintry 24 January, 1956, a former Caledonian Railway 4-4-0, no. 54462, heading a string of empty wagons, ambles past Gartsherrie North Junction in the complex of lines to the north of Coatbridge. Once used on express passenger trains to Carlisle and Aberdeen this engine had been relegated to local freight trips and was withdrawn for scrapping in 1960.

A 2-6-4T, no. 42689, leaving Drumpark Station, on the Rutherglen and Coatbridge line, with the 4.06 p.m. from Coatbridge (Central) to Balloch on 22 September, 1961. It is passing the former Drumpellier Junction which connected with an early mineral line serving the Monkland Canal.

The New Year Derby between Motherwell F.C. and Airdrieonians usually resulted in two or more football specials which, despite the relatively short mileage involved, took some forty minutes for the journey. On 2 January, 1956, a 'Black Five', no. 45309, arrives at Airdrie at 12.50 p.m. with the second train from Law Junction, the first train having been worked by a sister engine, no. 45485, which reversed direction at Gunnie Yard after traversing the freight spur at Whifflet which linked the former Caledonian and North British lines.

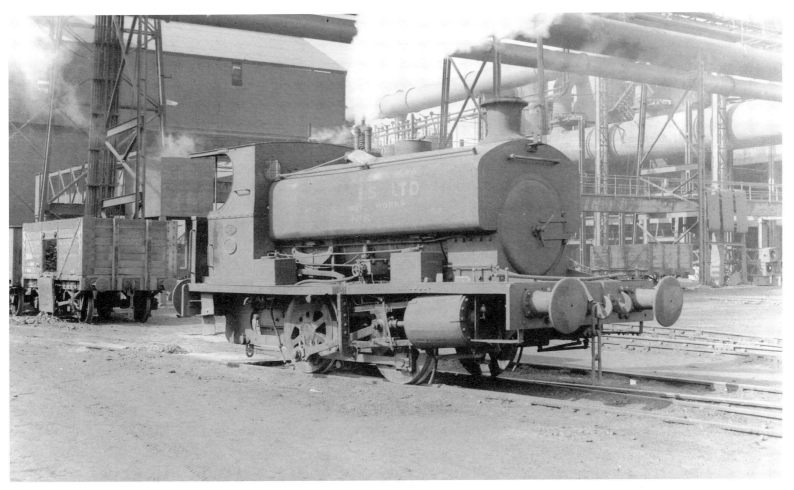

Apart from locomotives belonging to the main line railway companies, industrial Lanarkshire, with its collieries and iron, steel and engineering works, played host to perhaps as many as 700 shunting pugs over 150 years, the last of which (based at Bedlay Colliery) did not cease work until December, 1981. A few of these pugs were built by several small locomotive builders in the Airdrie area. In the 1950s Colville's Clyde Ironworks at Tollcross had a fleet of nine or more pugs and this 0-4-0 saddle tank, no. 8, built in 1899 by Andrew Barclay & Co. of Kilmarnock and modified in 1952, was photographed at the works on 10 July, 1954. The works, which were owned by James Dunlop & Co. until 1930, passed to the British Steel Corporation in 1970 and no longer exists.

A 'Black Five', no. 45476, calling at Bellshill on 25 April, 1963, with the 5.18 p.m. from Edinburgh (Princes Street) to Glasgow (Central). The station was another of those rebuilt at the turn of the century by the Caledonian Railway, a company whose progressive management would have been horrified by the running down of staffing and station facilities initiated by their successors.

The Chapelhall goods train was well known in enthusiast circles for being worked by Caledonian locomotives and for running on Saturday mornings. As Chapelhall was on the truncated Airdrie–Newhouse branch, which had closed in the 1930s, it was in later days reached by means of a mineral line from Bellside Junction at Cleland. This Pickersgill 0-6-0, no. 57689, was caught by the camera on 20 June, 1962, on the approach to Bellside Junction.

On 23 February, during the great freeze of early 1963, this 'Black Five', no. 44968, hurries across snow-covered moorland on the 1 in 99 climb from Shotts to Benhar summit with the 12.30 p.m. from Glasgow (Central) to Edinburgh (Princes Street). On a day of sub-zero temperatures the passengers were, no doubt, grateful for the train heating provided by a steam locomotive rather than a temperamental diesel, but by then steam had been all but eliminated from this former Caledonian route which in the pre-war days had provided the fastest services between the two cities.

Holytown Station on 20 July, 1963, in the days before bare platforms and plastic shelters. A class 6P Pacific, no. 72008, 'Clan Macleod' is passing through with the Glasgow portion of a Lourdes pilgrimage special from Folkestone.

The line from Holytown Junction to Law Junction was a useful link avoiding Motherwell and on 18 July, 1963, this standard class 5MT 4-6-0, no. 73057, was doing just that with an up freight.

Mossend Yard on a Spring or Summer evening was a favourite spot for railway photographers for, apart from freight train activity, the 'Limited Load' Royal Mail train (the number of vehicles conveyed was limited to allow for express running) from Aberdeen to Euston was followed by an express fish train. Both were normally worked by large passenger locos, as in this photograph taken on 1 May, 1963, of the postal headed by a class A2/3 Pacific, no. 60524, 'Herringbone', named after the racehorse that won the 1943 St Leger.

Photographed on the same evening, the up fish train had even more impressive power in the shape of the Coronation class Pacific, no. 46236, 'City of Bradford'.

The line between Motherwell and Hamilton, completed in 1876, includes a lofty viaduct over the River Clyde. In evening sunshine on 29 June, 1960, a class 4MT 2-6-0, no. 76113, crosses with a parcels van from Hamilton, a working made necessary by replacement of a locomotive hauled passenger train, to which the van had previously been attached, by a diesel multiple unit.

In the days of full employment, when Lanarkshire had an industrial based economy, annual works outings by rail were a regular feature and on 18 May, 1963, this train from Larkhall, the second of two, conveyed workers and their families to Glasgow to join the steamer *Queen Mary II* at Bridge Wharf for a cruise 'doon the watter'. The train was hauled by a pair of 'Black Fives', nos. 45008 and 45121, and is pictured passing the Bardykes Colliery branch, near Blantyre.

During the Second World War more than 1,000 khaki coloured 'Austerity' 2-8-0 locomotives were ordered by the Ministry of Supply for the War Department. Most were made by the North British Locomotive Co. which also turned out a ten coupled version. After the war, 733 of the 2-8-0s and twenty-five of the 2-10-0s were acquired by British Railways and this 2-10-0, no. 90770, was photographed on the evening of 2 July, 1955, clanking through Uddingston (Central) Station with an up train of empty wagons.

In the 1870s several influential coalmasters made a determined effort to break the Caledonian Railway monopoly of the Hamilton coalfield traffic and promoted the Glasgow, Bothwell, Hamilton & Coatbridge Railway. This ran from Shettleston (on the North British Railway) through Mount Vernon to Bothwell where there was a branch to Coatbridge; it then crossed the Clyde, passing through Uddingston to terminate at Hamilton. The North British soon took over and there were plans to extend to Motherwell, but with the working out of the Lanarkshire coalfield the line assumed a purely passenger role, being cut back to Bothwell in 1952 and closed completely three years later. On the last day of service, 2 July, 1955, this class V1 2-6-2T, no. 67698, is pictured at Uddingston (East) Station with the 3.56 p.m. train from Clydebank to Bothwell.

The village of East Kilbride was reached by the Busby Railway in 1868 and the branch was extended to High Blantyre in 1885, but this section was little used and closed in 1939. The new town at East Kilbride saved the remainder of the line from closure in 1964 and although the service had been basically deiselised in 1959 two peak period steam workings continued until March, 1966. This photograph shows a standard 2-6-4T, no. 80118, with one of those trains, the 5.33 p.m. from Glasgow (St Enoch), upon arrival at the somewhat rural looking terminus on 28 May, 1965.

Among lesser-known traffic conveyed by rail in years gone by were racing pigeons for release at predetermined locations. Photographed on 30 May, 1963, this 'Black Five', no. 45484, stands in Lesmahagow Station with one such train, the 7.20 p.m. from Coalburn to Carstairs via Rutherglen. Lesmahagow's railway viaduct was a prominent feature of the area, even after closure of the line in 1965, until its fairly recent demolition.

The mid-Lanark lines, completed in 1905 and with a life span of only some sixty years, formed a complex system centred on Stonehouse where on 23 August, 1955, this former Caledonian Railway 0-4-4T, no. 55182, arrived from Strathaven with a two coach train, itself indicative of declining patronage.

On 27 June, 1959, the 7.10 p.m. from Glasgow (Central) to Strathaven (Central) hauled by a 2-6-4T, no. 42058, passes Cot Castle, south of Stonehouse, the site of a never completed spur to the Coalburn line.

For many years Orangemen (and women!) travelled by train to their annual walks, held on the Saturday nearest to 12 July, commemorating the Battle of the Boyne. As many as twenty special trains could be required to go to a single venue and on 9 July, 1960, fifteen trains were required for a walk at Larkhall with nine using Larkhall Central Station and the others being dealt with at the former East Station, closed in 1951, which was temporarily reopened. The photograph shows a 2-6-4T, no. 42274, soon after leaving the latter station, with a 5.26 p.m. special returning to Bridgeton Cross.

On 13 September, 1963, the Coronation class Pacific, no. 46257, 'City of Salford' passes Jerviston Junction at the north end of Motherwell and approaches Braidhurst Viaduct with the 9.25 a.m. from Crewe to Perth. The train is conveying a horsebox, a style of traffic long since gone from the railways.

A typical engine shed scene of the steam days, photographed on 4 August, 1956, at Motherwell (still extant as a diesel depot) with a standard class 2MT 2-6-0, no. 78050, receiving some last minute attention before going off shed. At that period the shed housed around 106 locos with staff working in conditions largely unacceptable by today's standards.

Shieldmuir Junction was (and still is) a focal point for lines forming a Motherwell/Holytown/Wishaw triangle and, in the past, also spawned numerous private sidings for industrial establishments in the area. Photographed on 29 June, 1960, this 2-6-4T, no. 42271, is passing the signal box with empty coaches from Glasgow's Central Station *en route* to the carriage sidings at Law Junction.

A 'Black Five', no. 45099, pauses at Wishaw (Central) Station, situated on the loop from Shieldmuir Junction to Law Junction, with the 2.10 p.m. local from Carlisle to Glasgow (Central) on 19 August, 1958. There was also a Wishaw (South) Station, situated on the main line, but its service had been reduced to two trains each way daily and it was closed the following month.

At Law Junction the original main line and the Holytown loop (which was built after the main line had opened) part company. This Coronation 4-6-2, no. 46244, 'King George VI' is seen taking the main line with the 9.25 a.m. Crewe to Perth train on 27 May, 1963.

Craigenhill is a mini-summit situated between Braidwood and Cleghorn on the main line to Carlisle. On 20 October, 1962, this former Caledonian Railway 812 class 0-6-0, no. 57581, built in 1900, was making light work of the gradient with a railtour special starting from Glasgow (St Enoch) and taking in Chryston, Holytown, Muirkirk, Ayr Harbour and Greenock Princes Pier. The special was organised by the Scottish Locomotive Preservation Fund to help raise the sum of £900 deemed necessary by British Railways for purchase at scrap value of one of these locomotives for preservation. The fund raising effort proved successful and no. 57566 (built at St Rollox Works in Glasgow in 1899) was acquired in 1963. Restored to its original blue livery at Cowlairs Works, it was displayed for a number of years in the Glasgow Museum of Transport before going to the Strathspey Railway at Aviemore where, as Caledonian Railway no. 828, it can be seen at work. Craigenhill signal box was less fortunate, being closed in 1973 and demolished soon after.

On a bleak 11 February, 1956, a Caledonian 0-6-0, no. 57256, trundles past the old Caledonian station at Morningside with a loaded coal train from the Kingshill Collieries. Beyond the underbridge is the former North British station terminus of a straggling cross-country line from Bathgate in West Lothian and which was closed to passengers in 1930. The Caledonian station, also closed in 1930, was on a short-lived branch through Newmains from Cleland, but had access over a mineral line to Garriongill Junction on the Carlisle main line.

Photographed on 22 May, 1961, a pair of Caledonian veterans, Jumbo no. 57291 and 812 class no. 57620, are about to leave Kingshill No. 1 Colliery with forty wagons of coal for Clyde Ironworks. No. 57291 was the Morningside pilot and having banked the empty wagons to Kingshill, a moorland location near to the village of Allanton, it returned attached in front of the train engine to provide additional brake power on the descent to Morningside.

Less than two years later and the scene at Morningside had changed with the Caley veterans replaced by relatively modern British Railways standard class 2MT 2-6-0s. Photographed on 22 January, 1963, no. 78050 arrives with a loaded train from Kingshill.

In Spring sunshine a 'Black Five', no. 45459, one of 170 or so locomotives allocated to Glasgow's Polmadie depot, comes to a stand at Cleghorn Station on 15 April, 1961, with the 12.48 p.m. train from Lanark to Glasgow (Central). One or two passengers are leaving the train, while a family wait to board. With patronage at this level closure was inevitable in the Beaching era and came on 4 January, 1965, along with other small stations on the main line.

Lanark Junction, which had a triangular layout allowing direct access to the town from both Motherwell and Carstairs, is seen on 1 August, 1964, with a Jubilee class 4-6-0, no. 45705, 'Seahorse', passing southbound on the main line with empty coaching stock. The Carstairs side of the triangle has since been removed.

Through services between Edinburgh and Lanark ceased after 16 April, 1966, and for the last working on that bitterly cold evening St Margaret's Motive Power Depot at Edinburgh turned out the well-groomed B1 4-6-0, no. 61347. Lanark was on a former LMS line and as this engine was a former LNER style of locomotive it was a somewhat inappropriate choice for the 1845 departure from Waverley Station (the 24 hour clock was now used by BR) which is photographed upon arrival at Lanark. The train's previous starting point, Edinburgh Princes Street Station, had been closed in 1965.

Photographed earlier on the same day, this 'Black Five', no. 45309, runs into the deserted Carnwath Station with the 1630 from Lanark to Edinburgh.

From Dolphinton Junction (today known as Carstairs East) there was a little known branch line to the village of Dolphinton, but this had long since gone (in 1945) when this 'Black Five', no. 44793, was pictured passing the signal box on 27 October, 1962, hauling the 1.20 p.m. from Edinburgh (Princes Street) to Lanark.

A 2-6-4T, no. 42272, arrives at Auchengray Station with the 5.42 p.m. service from Edinburgh (Princes Street) to Lanark on 15 April, 1961. This was one of the small stations on what was initially termed the 'Edinburgh branch' from the Caledonian main line, but with some claim to importance as changing point for the Wilsontown branch. Another small claim to fame came during the very severe weather of early 1947 when the military (of which the author was one) were called in to clear the line from Auchengray to Cobbinshaw summit after heavy snowfalls. Unfortunately, meagre Army pay did not allow for photography at the scene!

On the grey morning of 1 October, 1960, this Coronation class Pacific, no. 46228 'Duchess of Rutland', pulls away from Carstairs with the 10.05 a.m. Glasgow (Central) to Birmingham. Of LMS design and dating back to 1937, these engines were known as 'Duchesses' among enthusiasts and considered by many to be the finest steam locomotives ever built in this country. Unfortunately, their illustrious career came to a premature end in 1964 owing, it was said, to British Railways top brass being incensed by footplate crews preferring them to the new diesel locomotives. Diesels were being built in large numbers at that time, but many crews had already concluded that these untried machines were underpowered and of suspect reliability.

A very typical steam age scene with the Jubilee class 4-6-0, no. 45706, 'Express', passing Carstairs on 15 April, 1961, heading a 10.15 a.m. relief express from Glasgow (Central) to London (Euston). The manual signalling, large signal box, numerous points and crossings and sidings full of wooden wagons were soon to be swept away by the modernisation plan.

Perhaps the locomotive most typical of the steam era in Lanarkshire was the 'Caley Jumbo', officially known as the British Railways class 2F 0-6-0. Two hundred and forty-four were built by the Caledonian Railway between 1883 and 1897, and until the early 1960s they could be seen pulling various trains from heavily laden coal freights to lightweight branch line passenger services. Inevitably, over the years various alterations were made to the appearance of the locos and this photograph of no. 57386, a Carstairs based engine, taken on 21 July, 1956, shows it with a short chimney.

The same engine photographed on the turntable at the Motive Power Depot at Carstairs on 1 October, 1960. By that time it had been given a longer and rather ugly stovepipe chimney.

Carstairs Motive Power Depot was built about 1850 and rebuilt by the LMS in 1935; by 1955 it had an allocation of thirty-six locomotives. Ten years later, despite the run down of steam power, it could still muster four of the ubiquitous 'Black Five' 4-6-0s, nos. 45492, 45171, 45309 and 44952, for a line up at the south end of the shed on 7 August, 1965.

An immaculate A4 Pacific, no. 60024, 'Kingfisher', basks in sunshine at Carstairs Motive Power Depot on 19 March, 1966. It was *en route* from its home shed of Aberdeen (Ferryhill) to Nine Elms, a former Southern Railway depot in south-east London, prior to working a railtour to Weymouth. By this time the A4s had been displaced from the East Coast main line by diesels and the dwindling band of survivors were employed on the three hour expresses between Glasgow (Buchanan Street) and Aberdeen. In 1938 the engine 'Mallard', which was of this class of loco, set the world speed record for steam traction at 126 m.p.h.

On 30 September, 1961, a class 6P Pacific, no. 72006, 'Clan Mackenzie', restarts from Symington with the 9.50 a.m. from London (Euston) to Perth. This station was the junction for the Peebles branch and, additionally, occasional Edinburgh connections from the south were made here rather than at Carstairs. The station was closed in 1965 and little trace remains.

The Wilsontown branch lost its meagre passenger service in 1951, but the intermediate station at Haywood came briefly to life on 30 September, 1961, when the ex-CR '19' class 0-4-4T, no. 55124, called with the Branch Line Society 'Pentland & Tinto Express' which also served Balerno and Biggar.

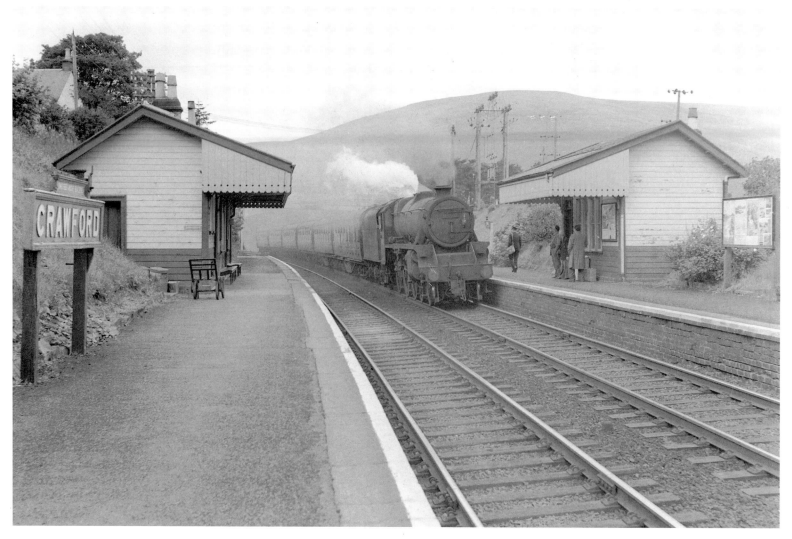

A 'Black Five', no. 45012, calls at the wayside station of Crawford on 1 August, 1964, with the 12.25 p.m. from Glasgow (Central) to Lockerbie. Closure of the station came five months later.